A VERY BRITISH COLOURING BOOK

CREATED BY WHITEBOX COLORING:

CREAM
CRACKERD

BUDGE
UP

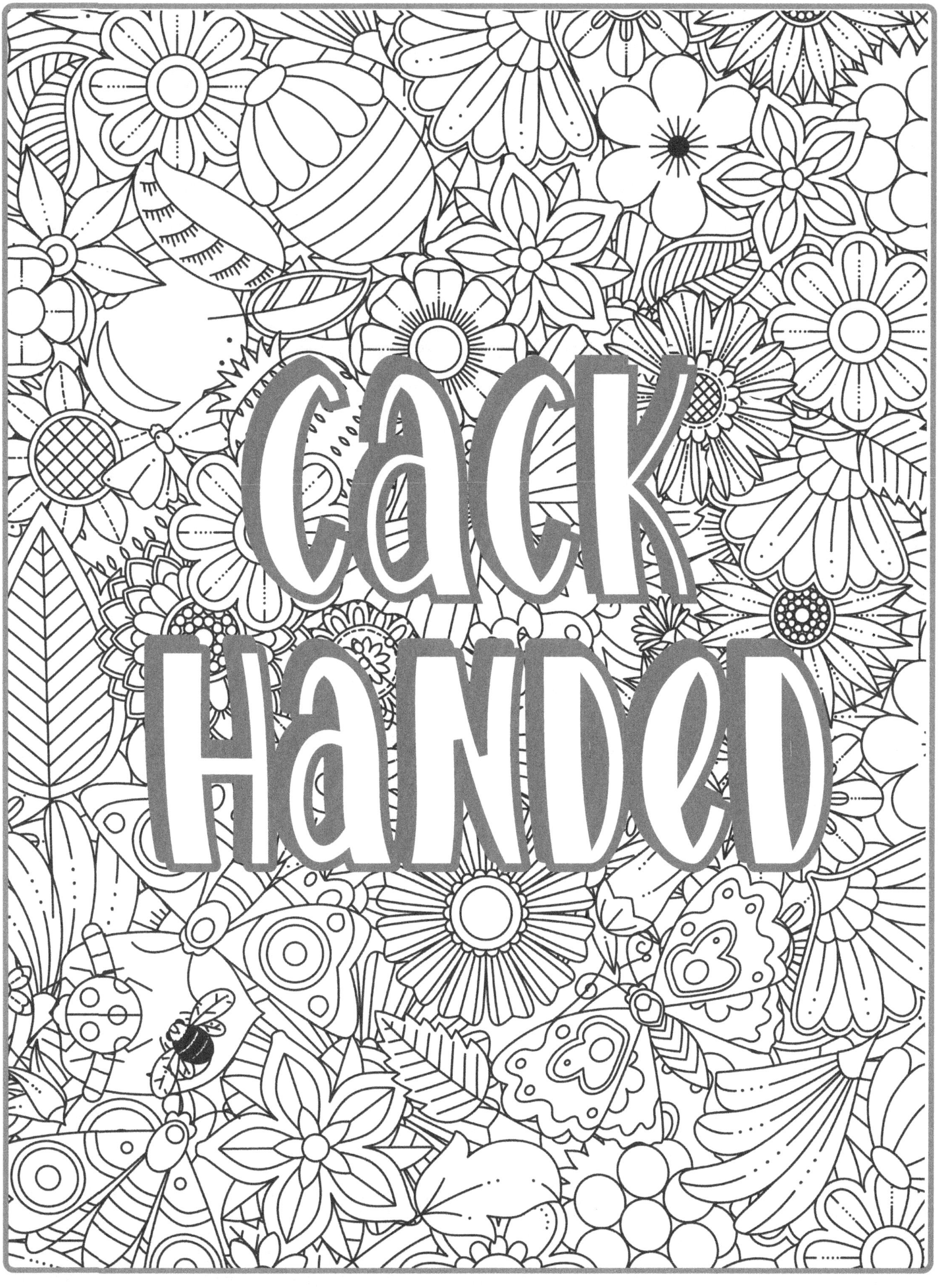
CACK
HANDED

PEAR
SHAPED

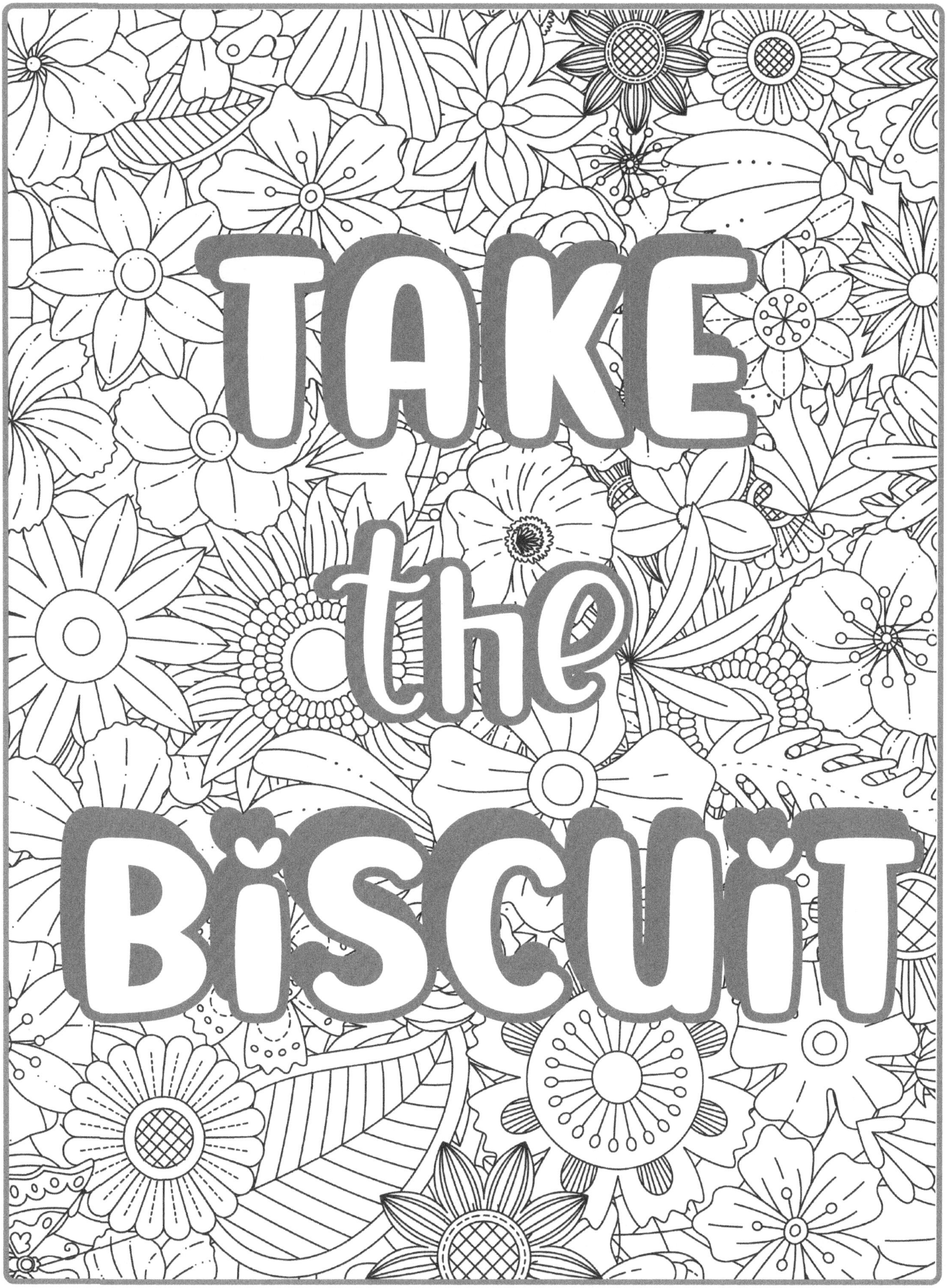
TAKE
the
BISCUIT

GOBSMACKED

BOG
STANDARD

SKEW
WIFF

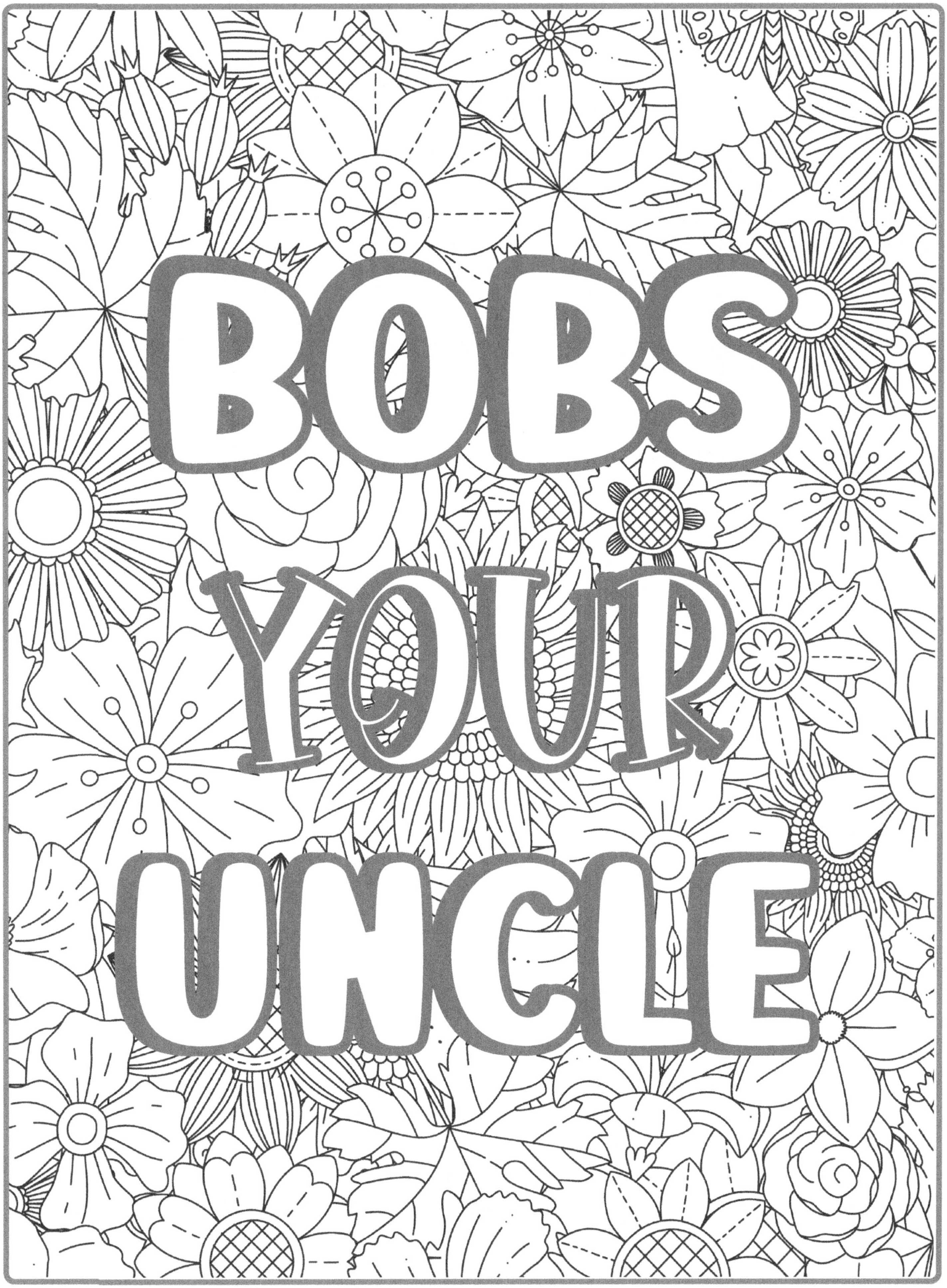
BOBS
YOUR
UNCLE

FULL
OF
BEANS

WIND
YOUR
NECK
IN

curtain
twitcher

DOG'S
DINNER

POP
YOUR
CLOGS

Bees
Knees

BOTCH
JOB

ON IT
Like A
CAR
Bonnet

GALLIVANTING

HANK
MARVIN

It's
A
SHAMBLES

tickety
BOO

GODSWALLOP

SPANNER
IN the
WORKS

SODS
LAW